Dörte Bluhm | Thomas Grundner

Bad Doberan Heiligendamm

Translation: Christiane Tümmler, Emilia Endler

HINSTORFF

Cover: Blick auf Heiligendamm
Cover: View of Heiligendamm

Seite 1: Eine Skulptur am Münster erinnert an den Schwan, der laut Legende maßgeblich für das Entstehen von Doberan war.
Page 1: A sculpture at the Minster reminds of the swan that played a substantial role in the founding of Doberan according to the legend.

Seite 2: Seit mehr als 200 Jahren gehören zwei Pavillons im Stil chinesischer Teehäuschen zum Kamp.
Page 2: For more than 200 years, two pavilions in the style of Chinese teahouses have been part of the Kamp.

Seiten 70/71: Von Herbstnebel und Dampfschwaden des „Molli" eingehüllte Landschaft
Pages 70/71: Autumnal scenery enveloped in fog and the steam clouds of the "Molli"

Rückcover: Das Doberaner Münster von Nordwesten gesehen
Backcover: The Doberan Minster seen from the northwest

Die Deutsche Nationalbibliothek verzeichnet diese Publikation in der Deutschen Nationalbibliografie; detaillierte bibliografische Daten sind im Internet unter http://dnb.de abrufbar.

Lagerstraße 7, 18055 Rostock
Tel.: 0381 4969-0
www.hinstorff.de

1. Auflage 2023

Herstellung: Hinstorff Verlag GmbH
Lektorat: Thomas Gallien
Übersetzungen: Emilia Endler, Christiane Tümmler
Karte: Claudia Trost
Layout: Iris Eschmann
Druck und Bindung: Westermann Druck Zwickau
Printed in Germany
ISBN 978-3-356-02446-3

Blick von Südwesten über Bad Doberan mit dem über 650 Jahre alten Münster im historischen Zentrum. Es wurde einst von Zisterziensermönchen errichtet und gilt heute als „Perle der Backsteingotik". Der hufeisenförmige Erweiterungsbau des Gymnasiums „Friderico Francisceum" (rechts) zeigt, dass es auch gelungene moderne Bauten in der Stadt gibt.

View over Bad Doberan from the southwest with the 650-year-old Minster in its center. It was built by Cistercian monks and today is considered a "pearl of the Brick Gothic". The horseshoe-shaped extension of the secondary school "Friderico Francisceum" (on the right) shows that there are successful modern buildings in town.

Anfänge im Morast

Der Legende nach war es ein Schwan, der mit seinem Ruf „dobr, dobr" – slawisch für „gut" – dafür sorgte, dass in der Nähe des späteren Bad Doberan, in Althof, einst ein Kloster entstand: Mecklenburgs Fürst Pribislav (gest. 1179) soll bei einer Jagd verkündet haben, dass er an der Stelle ein Kloster bauen lassen wolle, an der er den ersten Hirsch erlegen werde. Das Tier brach allerdings in morastigem Gelände zusammen, was dem Vorhaben nicht sonderlich zuträglich schien. Mit seinem „dobr, dobr" aber habe der vorbeifliegende Schwan den Fürsten in seinem Versprechen bestärkt. Aus „dobr" wurde Doberan, und bis heute gehören Hirsch und Schwan zum Stadtwappen.

Soweit die Legende. Historisch belegt ist, dass Pribislav das Kloster 1171 auf Empfehlung des Zisterzienserordens gründete. Dem Bau war aber nur eine kurze Lebensdauer beschert, denn schon 1179 wurde er beim letzten großen Slawenaufstand zerstört; die Ruine der Klosterscheune steht noch heute. Doch der fürstliche Wunsch nach einer Christianisierung des Landes war groß, und so wuchs bereits ab 1186 nur drei Kilometer entfernt die heutige Klosteranlage empor. Das zugehörige Dorf Doberan wurde 1177 erstmals schriftlich als *Villa Slavica Doberan* erwähnt – als Ort mit slawischen Bewohnern also.

Die Mönche des Doberaner Zisterzienserklosters kamen zunächst aus Amelungsborn im Weserbergland. Mit ihnen und den christlichen Siedlern aus Westfalen und Niedersachsen hielt in der von Wald geprägten Region zwischen Rostock und Wismar der Fortschritt Einzug. Die altansässigen Slawen profitierten nun von den Kenntnissen der Neuankömmlinge in Ackerbau, Handwerk und Medizin. Der Preis war der nicht immer freiwillige Übertritt zum Christentum.

Das Doberaner Kloster wurde schnell zum mächtigsten in Mecklenburg und konnte zeitweilig bis zu 66 Dörfer und Güter sein Eigen nennen. Auf eine romanische Vorgängerkirche folgte ab 1280 das größere Münster, das 1368 seine Schlussweihe erhielt und heute als „Perle der Backsteingotik" gilt. Es besticht durch Architektur und Ausstattung und zählt mit seinem 78 Meter langen Mittelschiff samt Kapellenkranz, dem 39 Meter langen Querschiff, einer Gewölbehöhe von bis zu 26,5 Metern sowie mit 24 gleichartigen Pfeilern zu den beeindruckendsten Kirchenbauten im Ostseeraum. Den mittelalterlichen Baumeistern war es gelungen, die Vorbilder des französischen Kathedralbaus und der norddeutschen Backsteinarchitektur mit dem Gebot der zisterziensischen Einfachheit zu vereinen. Letzterem ist das Fehlen eines Turms geschuldet. Europaweit heute einmalig ist die erhaltene hochgotische Ausstattung eines Zisterzienserklosters. Für seine Bedeutung spricht auch, dass das Kloster als Grablege der dänischen Königin Margarete (gest. 1282 in Rostock) diente und im Mittelalter Hauptbegräbnisstätte des Mecklenburger Fürstenhauses war.

Trotz aller Wirren der Zeit, trotz der Kriege und der Reformation und auch trotz zahlreicher, dem jeweiligen Geschmack geschuldeter Umbauten blieben mehrere Teile der Klosteranlage erhalten und konnten seit den 1960er-Jahren saniert werden: neben dem Münster auch das oktogonale Beinhaus (errichtet um 1250), das Kornhaus (um 1280) und das Brauhaus (um 1290). Eingefasst ist das um 1800 zum englischen Garten umgestaltete Areal nach wie vor von einer um 1290 errichteten, rund 1400 Meter langen Backsteinmauer. Bis heute sind die Sanierungs- und Restaurierungsarbeiten nicht abgeschlossen.

Beginnings in the mire

According to legend, it was a swan with its call of "dobr, dobr"(Slavic for good) that ensured the creation of a monastery in the vicinity of what is now Bad Doberan, in Althof: It is said that Mecklenburg's Prince Pribislav (died 1179) announced while hunting that he would have a monastery build on the spot where he first killed a deer. But the animal collapsed in marshy ground, which did not seem particularly favorable for the project. However, the passing swan with its "dobr, dobr" encouraged the prince in his promise. The word "dobr" became Doberan, and the stag and swan are still part of the town's coat of arms today.

So much for the legend. It is historically documented that Pribislav founded the monastery in 1171 on the advice of the Cistercian Order. The building had a short lifespan, as it was destroyed in the last major Slavic uprising in 1179. The ruins of the monastery's barn still stand today. Nevertheless, the prince's desire for the Christianization of the land was strong, and as a result, the current monastery complex rose just three kilometers away starting in 1186. The associated village of Doberan was first mentioned in writing in 1177 as *Villa Slavica Doberan* – a place with Slavic inhabitants.

The monks of the Doberan Cistercian monastery initially came from Amelungsborn in the Weserbergland region. Along with them and the Christian settlers from Westphalia and Lower Saxony, progress arrived in the forested region between Rostock and Wismar. The native Slavs now benefited from the knowledge of the newcomers in agriculture, crafts, and medicine. The price was the not always voluntary conversion to Christianity.

The Doberan monastery quickly became the most powerful in Mecklenburg and could at times call up to 66 villages and estates its own. Following a Romanesque predecessor church, the larger cathedral was built from 1280, receiving its final consecration in 1368 and today is considered a "pearl of brick Gothic". It stands out for its architecture and furnishings and is one of the most impressive church buildings in the Baltic Sea region with its 78 meter long central nave surrounded by a ring of chapels, the 39 meter long transept, a vault height of up to 26.5 meters and 24 similar pillars. The medieval builders had succeeded in combing the models of French cathedral building and North German brick architecture with the Cistercian virtue of simplicity. The lack of a tower is due to the latter. The preserved high Gothic furnishings of a Cistercian monastery are unique in Europe today. The monastery's importance is also demonstrated by its role as the burial place of Danish Queen Margarete (died 1282 in Rostock) and as the main burial site of the Mecklenburg dynasty in the Middle Ages.

Despite all the turmoil of the times, despite the wars and the Reformation, and also despite numerous alterations due to the respective taste, several parts of the monastery complex have been preserved and could be renovated since the 1960s: in addition to the cathedral, also the octagonal ossuary (built around 1250), the granary (around 1280) and the brewery (around 1290). The area, which was transformed into an English Garden around 1800, is still enclosed by a brick wall built around 1290 and about 1400 meters long. To date, the renovation and restoration work has not been completed.

Die Ruine der Klosterscheune in Althof zeugt bis heute von der Besiedlung Mecklenburgs durch deutsche Christen im 12./13. Jahrhundert.
The ruins of the monastery barn in Althof are testimony of the colonization of Mecklenburg by German Christians in the 12th and 13th century.

Seite 11: Die Kapelle Althof geht im Kern bis auf die Zeit um 1400 zurück. Ihr heutiges Aussehen erhielt sie 1886/88.
Page 11: The core of the chapel in Althof dates back to the time around 1400. It was given its present appearance in 1886/88.

Das Doberaner Münster war Mittelpunkt des bedeutenden, zwischen 1186 und 1552 bestehenden Zisterzienserklosters. Es zählt zu den eindrucksvollsten Kirchenbauten im Ostseeraum und ist als ein Höhepunkt auf der Europäischen Route der Backsteingotik jährlich das Ziel tausender Touristen – die an den Resten des Kreuzgangs vorbei durch das Eingangsportal (Seite 14) in den Innenraum treten. Dieses Portal befindet sich im Südflügel. Ein hoher Kirchturm fehlt, da er dem Gebot der zisterziensischen Schlichtheit widersprochen hätte. Dies ändert nichts daran, dass das Bauwerk imposant wirkt (Seite 15, Blick von Norden). In den 1960er- bis 1980er-Jahren wurde der Bau nach 1882 bis 1889 zum zweiten Mal umfassend restauriert. Zwischen 2001 und 2018 folgte eine dritte große Sanierung.

The Doberan Minster was the center of the important Cistercian abbey existing between 1186 and 1552. It is one of the most impressive churches in the Baltic Sea region and attracts thousands of tourists each year as a highlight of the European Route of Brick Gothic. The visitors enter the interior of the Minster through the porch passing the remains of the cloister (page 14). This porch is located in the south wing. There is no high steeple because it would have been contrary to the Cistercian rule of simplicity. However, that does not keep this building from being impressive (page 15, view from the north). The church was extensively restored three times: From 1882 to 1889, in the 1960s to 1980s, and between 2001 and 2018.

Der monumentale Kreuzaltar von 1360/70 besteht aus einem zweiseitigen Flügelaltar, über dem sich das 15 Meter hohe Triumphkreuz befindet.

The monumental cross altar from 1360/70 is a double-sided wing altar with a triumphal cross 15 meters high on top of it.

Seite 16: Der Hochaltar aus den Jahren kurz nach 1300 ist mit großer Sicherheit der älteste erhaltene Flügelaltar der Welt. Er ist vier Meter hoch, der höchste Fialenturm ragt bis in sechs Meter Höhe. Der links im Altarraum aufgestellte Sakramentsturm erreicht sogar 11,60 Meter.

Page 16: The high altar was created shortly after 1300 and is most likely the oldest extant wing altar in the world. It is four meters high, the tallest pinnacle rising up to a height of six meters. The tabernacle standing on the left in the choir even reaches 11.60 meters in height.

Die 26 Meter Gewölbehöhe fallen im Vergleich mit anderen Kirchen der Backsteingotik – etwa in Lübeck (St. Marien, 38,5 Meter), Wismar (St. Nikolai, 37 Meter), Rostock (St. Marien, 31,5 Meter) und Stralsund (St. Marien, 32,9 Meter) – fast bescheiden aus. Trotzdem beeindrucken sie bei jedem Besuch aufs Neue!

The vault with its 26 meters in height seems modest compared to other Brick Gothic churches like the ones in Lübeck (St Mary's, 38.5 meters), Wismar (St Nicolas', 37 meters), Rostock (St Mary's, 31.5 meters) and Stralsund (St Mary's, 32.9 meters). Nevertheless, it impresses anew at every visit!

Das Münster und der umgebende Park sind zauberhaft – nicht nur bei schräg einfallendem, letzten Nebel vertreibendem Sonnenlicht.
The Minster and the surrounding park are charming – not only when the fog is slowly lifted by the oblique illumination of the sunlight.

Das Küsterhaus wird heute privat genutzt.
The sexton's house is now privately used.

Seite 22: Blick vom südlichen Querschiff auf das Küsterhaus (nach 1830 gebaut), das einstige Kornhaus (ab 1293) und die Ruine des ehemaligen Wirtschaftshauses (um 1290, Brand 1979).
Page 22: View from the southern transept over the sexton's house (built after 1830), the former grain storage (from 1293) and the ruins of the former trade building (from 1290, burnt in 1979).

Rechts oben: Bis heute fasst die um 1290 errichtete 1400 Meter lange Backsteinmauer das Areal des ehemaligen Klosters ein.

Top right: The 1400 meters of brick wall, built in 1290, enclose the grounds of the former abbey.

Seite 24: Ins oktogonale Beinhaus aus den Jahren um 1250 wurden die Gebeine verstorbener Klosterbrüder aufgenommen, damit deren Gräber neu belegt werden konnten. Gleich daneben befand sich einst der Mönchsfriedhof.

Page 24: The octagonal charnel house from around 1250 was the resting place of the bones of deceased friars in order to reuse their graves. The cemetery for the monks used to be right next to it.

Rechts unten: Auf Bänken im Park und unter den Resten des Kreuzganges kann man die besondere Atmosphäre rund um das Doberaner Münster in Ruhe auf sich wirken lassen.

Bottom right: The benches in the park and under the remains of the cloister are ideal for enjoying the special atmosphere around the Doberan Minster in peace.

Ein mittelalterliches Kloster war ein religiöses, aber auch ein wirtschaftliches Zentrum. Zeugnisse davon finden sich noch heute in Bad Doberan. Zu den Apfelsorten, die auf dem Klostergelände wachsen, gehört die „Reinette". Diese uralte Sorte wurde einst von Mönchen aus Frankreich an die Ostsee gebracht. Die Woll- oder Wolfsscheune vom Ende des 13. Jahrhunderts, mittlerweile eine Ruine (Seite 26), diente zunächst vermutlich als Hospital und war später Arbeits- und Vorratshaus sowie Wollmanufaktur.

A medieval monastery was a religious yet economic center proof of which can still be found in Bad Doberan. One of the apple cultivars growing on the abbey's grounds is the "Reinette". This ancient cultivar was once brought to the Baltic coast from France by monks. The Wollscheune or Wolfsscheune (the wool barn or wolf barn) from the late 13th century, now in ruins (page 26), was presumably first used as a hospital and later became a workshop, a storage room, and a wool manufactory.

Hinter dem früheren Kornhaus, das auch als Pferdestall und Stadtschule diente und heute als soziokulturelles Zentrum genutzt wird, wurde 2002 ein Klostergarten angelegt. Er beherbergt rund 100 Arten an Kräutern, Heil- und Würzpflanzen.

The former grain storage was also used as a horse stable and the town's school and is now a sociocultural center. Behind it, a monastery garden was created in 2002 which contains about 100 kinds of herbs and medicinal plants.

Oben: Das Torhaus aus dem Jahr 1763, gleich neben dem Westtor (Seite 31) der Klosteranlage, wurde 2007/08 saniert und lädt seitdem im Café zum Verweilen und im kleinen Laden zum Stöbern ein.

Top: The Torhaus (Gatehouse) from 1763 is located right next to the Western Gate (page 31) of the monastery complex. It was restored in 2007/08 and since invites visitors to linger at a café and a little shop.

Unten: Das Amtshaus, Ende des 18. Jahrhunderts errichtet, ist ein prächtiger Fachwerkbau, der auch schon als Schule und als Arbeitsamt diente. Nach dem Kauf und der Sanierung durch die Evangelisch-Lutherische Kirchgemeinde Bad Doberan beherbergt das Gebäude seit 2014 einen großen Saal und dient dem Gemeindeleben.

Bottom: The Amtshaus (Official Building), constructed at the end of the 18th century, is a splendid half-timbered house which has already been used as a school and an employment office. After the Lutheran-Protestant parish of Bad Doberan bought and restored the building, it now houses a great hall and serves the community life since 2014.

TORHAUS
TORHAUS
Café
KLOSTERLADEN

Kleine Pfade führen durch den Klosterpark, Holzbrücken überspannen kleine Wasserläufe.

Narrow paths lead through the abbey's park, and wooden bridges span small watercourses.

Seite 31: Blick durch das Westtor in die um 1910 errichtete Beethovenstraße. Das Tor trennte einst das Klostergelände von der Außenwelt. Auf dem vorgelagerten Platz versammelten sich Pilger zu Andachten, erhielten Bedürftige Essen.

Page 31: View of the street Beethovenstraße, built around 1910, through the Westtor (Western Gate). It once separated the monastery grounds from the outside world. The square in front of the gate was a place for pilgrims to gather for prayer services, and for the poor to receive food.

Im Winter kann die einstige Abgeschiedenheit des Zisterzienserklosters besonders gut nachempfunden werden.
The seclusion of the former Cistercian abbey can be felt especially in winter.

Vom herzoglichen Bad zum Gipfel-Strandkorb

Die Staats- und Regierungschefs der acht wichtigsten Industrienationen vereint in einem XXL-Strandkorb – das Foto ging 2007 um die Welt. Deutschland war damals für das Gipfeltreffen verantwortlich und hatte sich für Heiligendamm als Tagungsort entschieden.

Dass die damalige Kanzlerin Angela Merkel in ihr Heimat-Bundesland einlud, lag nahe; dass die Wahl auf Heiligendamm fiel, hatte sicher mit dem einmaligen Bauensemble zu tun. Nach jahrzehntelangem Verfall zu DDR-Zeiten war dessen Pracht 2007 bereits in einigen Teilen wieder sichtbar. Die Kölner Fundus-Gruppe unter Anno August Jagdfeld hatte den Ortskern 1996 für 18 Millionen DM vom Bundesvermögensamt erworben und anschließend fünf Gebäude restauriert. 2003 eröffnete die Kempinski-Gruppe ein 5-Sterne-plus-Haus.

Das Projekt stieß nicht überall auf Gegenliebe, zudem hatten mehrere Akteure verschiedene Auffassungen von der Weiterentwicklung des Hotels und des historischen Ortskerns. Es kam zu Planänderungen und Verkäufen. Heute ist das Grand Hotel Heiligendamm ein eigenständiges Unternehmen; die Sanierung weiterer historischer Gebäude und mehrere Neubauten erfolgen sukzessive unter der Ägide von Anno August Jagdfeld.

Den besten Blick auf die grandiose „Weiße Stadt am Meer" hat man von der Ostsee – von einem der Fahrgastschiffe, die zwischen Kühlungsborn und Rostock unterwegs sind; von einem Motor- oder Segelboot, das in einer der Marinas gechartert werden kann; beim Surfen oder Kitesurfen. Und auch die 200 Meter lange Seebrücke bietet herrliche Aussichten. Einige Bereiche der historischen Anlagen sind allerdings nicht frei zugänglich.

In Bad Doberan ist der Kamp wie vor 200 Jahren das touristische Zentrum des Ortes. Rings um den Park strahlen die sanierten historischen Gebäude wie etwa das Großherzogliche Palais und das Salongebäude, das Prinzenpalais, das Haus Gottesfrieden und das Haus Medini. Viele laden als Hotel, Verwaltungsgebäude oder Veranstaltungsort auch zum Betreten ein. Die Gassen der Innenstadt werden von zahlreichen kleinen Läden gesäumt, in denen oft Handwerkliches und Kulinarisches aus der Region angeboten werden – die einstige herzogliche Sommerresidenz ist in den vergangenen 30 Jahren zu einer neuen Blüte gekommen.

Nah beim Münster steht das frühere Kornhaus der Zisterziensermönche. Es ist eines der ältesten erhaltenen Gebäude seiner Art in Norddeutschland und dient heute als soziokulturelle Stätte. Der älteste noch erhaltene weltliche Bau von Bad Doberan ist das 1763 errichtete und 1888 umgebaute Torhaus, heute Klosterladen und Café.

Von der wechselvollen Geschichte des Ortes erzählt das Stadt- und Bädermuseum im Möckelhaus. Benannt ist es nach dem einst über Mecklenburg hinaus bekannten Architekten Gotthilf Ludwig Möckel, der es 1886 bis 1888 für sich als Wohnhaus errichtete.

Und was ist mit dem Bäderwesen, das Doberan und Heiligendamm vor 230 Jahren überhaupt erst prosperieren ließ? Bis heute locken mildes Reizklima, Ostseewasser und Moorbäder Tausende Patienten und Kurgäste an. An die Stelle der Badehäuser sind zwei Kurkliniken sowie Gesundheits- und Wellnessanbieter getreten. Aus der herzoglichen Sommerfrische sind zwei moderne Kur- und Erholungsorte geworden.

From the ducal bath to the summit beach chair

The heads of state and government of the eight most important industrial nations united in an XXL beach chair — the photo went around the world in 2007. At the time, Germany was responsible for the summit and had chosen Heiligendamm as the venue.

It was only appropriate that the then Chancellor, Angela Merkel, invited the guests to her home state. The choice of Heiligendamm was surely influenced by the unique ensemble of architectural buildings. After decades of decay during the GDR era, some of its splendor was already visible again in 2007. The Cologne Fundus Group under Anno August Jagdfeld had acquired the village center from the Federal Property Office in 1996 for DM 18 million and subsequently restored five buildings. In 2003, the Kempinski Group opened a 5-star-plus hotel.

The project did not meet with approval everywhere; moreover, several stakeholders had different views on the economic and structural further development of the hotel and the historic town center. This led to changes in plans and sales. Today, the Grand Hotel Heiligendamm is an independent company; the renovation of further historic buildings and several new buildings are successively taking place under the aegis of Anno August Jagdfeld.

The best view of the grandiose "White Town by the Sea" is from the Baltic Sea: from one of the passenger ships that travel between Kühlungsborn and Rostock; from a motorboat or sailboat that can be chartered in one of the marinas; while surfing or kite surfing. And the 200-meter-long pier also offers magnificent views. However, some areas of the historic facilities are not freely accessible.

In Bad Doberan, the Kamp is the tourist center of the town, as it was 200 years ago. Its two pavilions, once built in Chinese style, house a gallery and a café. Around the park shine the renovated historic buildings such as the Grand Ducal Palace and the Salon Building, the Princes' Palace, the House Gottesfrieden and the House Medini. Many invite visitors to enter: as hotels, administrative buildings or event venues. The alleys of the city center are lined with numerous small stores, often offering handicrafts and culinary delights from the region – the former ducal summer residence has blossomed again in the past 30 years.

Close to the Minster stands the former granary of the Cistercian monks. It is one of the oldest preserved buildings of its kind in northern Germany and today serves as a sociocultural site. The oldest surviving secular building in Bad Doberan is the Torhaus, built in 1763 and rebuilt in 1888, now a monastery store and café.

The Town and Resort Museum in the Möckelhaus tells of the eventful history of the town. It is named after the architect Gotthilf Ludwig Möckel, who was once known beyond the borders of Mecklenburg and who built it for himself as a residence between 1886 and 1888.

And what about the spa industry that allowed Doberan and Heiligendamm to prosper in the first place 230 years ago? To this day, the mild, stimulating climate, Baltic Sea water and mud baths attract thousands of patients and spa guests. The bathhouses have been replaced by two spa clinics and health and wellness providers. The ducal summer resort has become two modern health-and-recreation resorts.

Oben: Bis etwa 1795 diente der Friedhof am Kloster als städtische Ruhestätte. Der danach eingerichtete, bis heute genutzte neue Friedhof Bad Doberan liegt etwas außerhalb des Stadtzentrums.

Top: The cemetery at the abbey was used as a municipal last resting-place until about 1795. After that, the new cemetery of Bad Doberan was installed which is still used and located somewhat out of town.

Unten und Seite 39: Die Beethovenstraße grenzt an das Klostergelände und ist Standort prächtiger Stadtvillen (links). An ihr liegt auch das Möckelhaus (Seite 39), einstiges Domizil des Architekten Gotthilf Ludwig Möckel. Der im neogotischen Stil errichtete Bau beherbergt heute das Stadt- und Bädermuseum.

Botton and page 31: The street Beethovenstraße abuts the monastery grounds and is the site of magnificent mansions (on the left), for example, the Möckelhaus (page 39) which once was the residence of the architect Gotthilf Ludwig Möckel. The Neo-Gothic building now houses the Town and Resort Museum.

MUSEUM
Café & Klosterladen
TORHAUS

Der zweistöckige weiße Pavillon und der etwas kleinere gelbe Pavillon, beide im chinesischen Stil gebaut, gehören seit 1808/09 zum Doberaner Kamp. Ihr Architekt Carl Theodor Severin entsprach damit der Liebe Friedrich Franz I. für fernöstliche Motive. Die parkartige Anlage mit ihren alten Eichen wird seit über 200 Jahren zum Erholen genutzt.

The two-story white pavilion and the slightly smaller yellow pavilion, both built in the Chinese style, are part of the Doberan Kamp since 1808/09. Their architect Carl Theodor Severin thus satisfied Friedrich Franz I. who loved motifs of the Far East. The park-like site with its old oaks has been used for recreation for more than 200 years.

GALERIE
GALERIE
ROTER PAVILLON
Bruchstücke
PETER BAUER

Der betriebsame Alexandrinenplatz im Herzen Bad Doberans wurde nach Friederike Wilhelmine Alexandrine Marie Helene Prinzessin von Preußen (1803–1892) benannt, die durch ihre Heirat mit Paul Friedrich von Mecklenburg 1823 auch Erbgroßherzogin von Mecklenburg-Schwerin wurde.

The bustling square Alexandrinenplatz in the heart of Bad Doberan was named after Princess Friederike Wilhelmine Alexandrine Marie Helene of Prussia (1803–1892) who also became Hereditary Grand Duchess of Mecklenburg-Schwerin through her marriage with Paul Friedrich von Mecklenburg in 1823.

Das Friedrich-Franz-Palais (rechts), vollendet 1795, war eines der ersten Logierhäuser in Doberan. Auch heute dient es als Hotel und erinnert mit seinem Namen an den Begründer Doberans und Heiligendamms als Kur- und Badeorte. Das Salongebäude (hinten) entstand 1801/02 als Speise- und Gesellschaftshaus. Heute ist es ein Verwaltungsgebäude des Landkreises Rostock.

The palace Friedrich-Franz-Palais (on the right), completed in 1795, was one of the first Logierhäuser (guest houses) in Doberan. It still is a hotel today and bears the name of the founder of Doberan and Heiligendamm as seaside resorts. The Salongebäude (parlor building, in the back) was built in 1801/02 for dining and other social purposes. Today it is one of the administrative buildings of the Rostock district.

Mit Dampf an die Ostsee

Mit maximal 40 Stundenkilometern ist der „Molli“ nicht die schnellste, aber die schönste Möglichkeit, von Bad Doberan nach Heiligendamm zu gelangen. Die 900 mm-Schmalspurbahn wurde 1886 in Betrieb genommen, nachdem die immer zahlreicher werdenden Urlauber kaum noch per Pferdefuhrwerk über die Chaussee zwischen Doberan und Heiligendamm transportiert werden konnten.

Doberan selbst war seit der Eröffnung der Strecke Rostock–Wismar 1883 ans (inter-)nationale Bahnnetz angeschlossen. Für „de Berliners“, wie alle Urlauber aus Brandenburg und der Hauptstadt der Einfachheit halber oft genannt wurden, und für die Gäste aus Hamburg war das eine enorme Erleichterung der Anreise. Immer mehr Menschen zog es nun für die Sommerfrische an die Ostsee, weshalb der Großherzog im Juni 1886 den Bau einer Schmalspur-Verbindung nach Heiligendamm veranlasste. Die 6,6 Kilometer lange Strecke – es klingt unglaublich – ging bereits einen Monat später in Betrieb!

Wurden die Dampfloks auf den Hauptstrecken der Bahn im 20. Jahrhundert peu à peu aus dem Dienst genommen, überlebte der (nicht die!) „Molli“ zur Freude aller Nostalgie-Fans.

Ganz nach Gusto ist die Reise im Salonwagen erster Klasse auf roten Samtpolstern und bei Kaffee und Kuchen zu genießen, zweiter Klasse im Nostalgiewagen oder in der „Holzklasse“. Echte Dampflokliebhaber lassen sich auf den Perrons den Fahrtwind um die Nase wehen oder melden sich sogar für eine Fahrt neben Heizer und Lokführer an.

Der „Molli“ verkehrt ganzjährig, in der Urlaubssaison etwas häufiger als im Winter. Wenn er aus Bad Doberan kommend die Innenstadt hinter sich gelassen hat und dabei kaum durch die engen Gassen zu passen scheint, biegt er auf die Dammchaussee ein und zuckelt noch etwas an einigen Klinkerbauten vorbei. In der Nummer 23 hat lange Jahre der Schriftsteller Ehm Welk gelebt, der mit seinen auch verfilmten „Heiden von Kummerow“ eine Millionen-Auflage erreichte. Heute erinnert hier ein Literaturhaus an ihn.

Wenig später passiert die Schmalspurbahn die älteste deutsche Galopprennbahn. 1822 hatte man zu Ehren der Erbgroßherzogin Alexandrine erste Pferderennen organisiert, damals noch auf freiem Feld. Schon 1823 lud der eigens gegründete Doberaner Rennverein auf eine richtige Rennbahn ein – ein weiteres Highlight für die illustren Sommergäste.

Abgesehen von Unterbrechungen in den 1920er-Jahren und zwischen 1939 und 1945 lief der Betrieb bis Anfang der 1960er und dann wieder ab 1993. Mit der Corona-Pandemie kam alles erneut zum Erliegen.

Auf der anderen Seite der parallel zur L12 verlaufenden Gleise erstrecken sich eine Lindenallee und ein Waldstück. Beide lassen die „Molli“-Reise in jeder Jahreszeit zu einem unvergesslichen Erlebnis werden: Im Frühjahr strahlen die Anemonen wie ein weißes Sternenmeer und die Bäume zeigen erstes zartes Grün; im Sommer bilden die Baumkronen ein undurchdringliches Dach; im Oktober leuchtet alles in prächtigen Herbstfarben. Der Winter schließlich lässt die Landschaft klar und still erscheinen, nur das Stampfen und Pfeifen der Lok ist zu hören.

With steam to the Baltic Sea

With a maximum speed of 40 kilometers per hour, the „Molli“ is not the fastest but the most beautiful way to get from Bad Doberan to Heiligendamm. The 900 mm narrow-gauge railway was put into operation in 1886, after the ever-increasing number of vacationers could hardly be transported by horse-drawn carriage on the road between Doberan and Heiligendamm.

Bad Doberan itself had been connected to the (inter)national railway network since the opening of the Rostock–Wismar route in 1883. For the "de Berliners" as all vacationers from Brandenburg and the capital were often called for simplicity's sake, and for the guests from Hamburg, this was a tremendous easing of the journey. More and more people were now drawn to the Baltic Sea for the summer, which is why the Grand Duke ordered the construction of a narrow-gauge connection to Heiligendamm in June 1886. The 6.6-kilometer line – it sounds incredible – went into operation just one month later! While steam locomotives on main lines were gradually taken out of service in the 20th century, the "Molli" survived to the delight of all nostalgia fans.

The journey can be enjoyed according to taste in the first-class salon car on red velvet cushions and with coffee and cake, second class in the nostalgia car, or in the "wooden class". Real steam locomotive enthusiasts can have the wind blow around their noses on the platforms or even sign up for a ride alongside the stoker and locomotive driver.

The "Molli" operates all year round, more frequently during the holiday season than in winter. When it leaves Bad Doberan, having left the city center behind, and seems hardly be able to pass through the narrow streets, it turns onto the Dammchaussee and chugs past a few brick buildings. For many years, the writer Ehm Welk lived in number 23, he achieved a million-edition with his book "Heiden von Kummerow", which was also made into a successfully film. Today, a literature house here commemorates him.

Shortly after, the narrow-gauge railway passes the oldest German gallop racecourse. In 1822, horse races were organized in honor of the Hereditary Grand Duchess Alexandrine, at that time still on open field. As early as 1823, the newly founded Doberan Racing Club invited guests to a proper racecourse – another highlight for the illustrious summer guests.

Apart from interruptions in the 1920s and between 1939 and 1945, the operations continued until the early 1960s and then again from 1993. Due to the coronavirus pandemic, everything came to a halt again.

A linden avenue and a forest lie on the other side of the rails running parallel to the road L12. Both make the journey on the "Molli" unforgettable: In the spring, the anemones shine like a white sea of stars and the trees show the first hint of a pale green, in the summer, the treetops form an impenetrable roof, in October, everything glows in magnificent autumnal colors. And the winter makes the scenery seem clear and peaceful, only the pounding and whistling of the locomotive can be heard.

Bad Doberan als Veranstaltungsort: Seit 1990 feiern Frank Zappa-Fans ihr Idol bei der „Zappanale", mittlerweile eine Großveranstaltung, die auf der Galopprennbahn stattfindet (oben). 1998 gab es den ersten Biker-Gottesdienst im Münster, inzwischen reisen jährlich mehrere tausend Fans auf etwa 1500 Maschinen an (Seite 47).

Bad Doberan as a venue: Since 1990, fans or Frank Zappa celebrate their idol at the "Zappanale" which has become a big event by now and takes place on the racecourse (top). In 1998, the Minster offered the first service for bikers. Meanwhile, thousands of fans per year arrive on approximately 1500 motorcycles (page 47).

99 2323-6
ZONE

Eine der schönsten Alleen in Mecklenburg-Vorpommern erstreckt sich zwischen Bad Doberan und Heiligendamm. Die Bäume wurden um 1850 gepflanzt und erfreuen heute als eine der ältesten und längsten Lindenalleen Europas die Reisenden.
One of the most beautiful avenues in Mecklenburg-West Pomerania runs from Bad Doberan to Heiligendamm. The trees were planted around 1850 and delight travelers today as one of the oldest and longest linden avenues in Europe.

Seite 48: 1886 schnaufte der „Molli" erstmals von Doberan nach Heiligendamm, um Badegäste zu transportieren.
Page 48: In 1886, the steam train "Molli" brought resort guests from Doberan to Heiligendamm for the first time.

Der aus Heiligendamm kommende „Molli“ auf der Dammchaussee Richtung Bad Doberan: Sonne, Wald, nahes Meer, eine entschleunigte, romantische Form des Reisens. Das klingt nach Urlaub. Aber auch in der kalten Jahreszeit ist die Schmalspurbahn unterwegs.

The "Molli" coming from Heiligendamm on its way to Bad Doberan on a causeway: sun, woods, the close sea, a slow and romantic way to travel. That sounds like vacation. But the narrow-gauge railway is on the move in winter as well.

Im historischen Bahnhofsgebäude von Heiligendamm können Reisende auf den „Molli“ aus Bad Doberan und aus Kühlungsborn warten. Am Schalter ausgehändigte Pappfahrkarten lassen Nostalgie aufkommen, und im Restaurant „Herzoglicher Wartesaal“ kann man gediegen speisen.

In the historical railway building in Heiligendamm, travelers can wait for the "Molli" coming from Bad Doberan and Kühlungsborn. They can receive nostalgic paper tickets at the counter and eat well in the restaurant "Herzoglicher Wartesaal" ("Ducal Waiting Hall").

2
5
5

Baden am Heiligen Damm

Mit der Reformation setzte der Niedergang des Doberaner Klosters und des umliegenden Ortes ein. Während die Kirche die Zeit als evangelisches Gotteshaus überdauerte, verfielen zahlreiche andere Gebäude und auch das Dorf durchlebte Kriege und Seuchen mehr schlecht als recht. Erst als Residenzort gewann Doberan ab 1793/94 wieder an Bedeutung, wurde 1879 zur Stadt und 1929 zum „Bad".

Auslöser war die Empfehlung des herzoglichen Leibarztes, aus gesundheitlichen Gründen im Meer zu baden und deshalb am Heiligen Damm ein Badehaus zu errichten. Heiligendamm, wie der Ort später hieß, wurde so 1793 zum ersten deutschen Seebad. Herzog Friedrich Franz I. wollte sich jedoch nicht nur seiner Gesundheit, sondern auch dem Vergnügen widmen und ließ im benachbarten Doberan eine Sommerresidenz entstehen.

In Heiligendamm wuchs bis 1870 ein einzigartiges klassisch-romantisches Gesamtkunstwerk aus Bade- und Logierhäusern heran, das über Jahrzehnte den europäischen Hochadel inklusive der russischen Zarenfamilie anzog, firmiert und 2007 Austragungsort des G8-Gipfels war. Zentrum des Ensembles war und ist das Kurhaus mit dem Ballsaal heute Restaurant des Grand Hotels. Direkt daneben liegt das einstige Badehaus, heute als Haus Mecklenburg in das Grand Hotel integriert. Nach Westen schließen sich die Burg Hohenzollern, gleichfalls zum Grand Hotel gehörend, sowie drei Cottages im englischen Landhausstil an – inzwischen Appartementhäuser beziehungsweise noch unsaniert. Östlich des Kurhauses entstanden acht Logierhäuser, die mittlerweile zum Teil saniert sind und als Appartements genutzt werden. Auch die als Ladenzeile errichteten Kolonnaden sind in Privatbesitz, die Orangerie wiederum nutzt das Grand Hotel.

Auch in Doberan wurde gebaut, etwa das heutige Kurhaus, das Amtshaus, das Salongebäude, ein nicht mehr erhaltenes Theater, zwei Pavillons im chinesischen Stil, das Großherzogliche Palais, das Sanatorium Stahlbad (später Moorbad, mittlerweile Ruine) und das Prinzenpalais. Im neogotischen Stil entstanden unter anderem das heutige Stadtmuseum (1887/88) und das Gymnasium.

In den ersten Jahren wohnten die Gäste in Doberan und fuhren nur zum Baden nach Heiligendamm. Damen und Herren waren getrennte Bereiche zugewiesen, man ließ sich gemeinhin in Badekarren ein paar Meter in die See ziehen und stieg von einer kleinen Treppe aus ins Wasser. Auch das Amüsement gehörte zum Aufenthalt: die Anreise per Kutsche, das Sehen und Gesehen-Werden, Spaziergänge, Konzerte und Bootsfahrten. Zurück in Doberan folgten nachmittags Spaziergänge über den Kamp, ein Besuch der Spielbank oder der Modegeschäfte. Der Abend gehörte dem Theater, den Bällen oder Gesellschaften.

Schnell entstanden jedoch auch direkt in Heiligendamm Cottages, Hotels, Logierhäuser und Pensionen, in denen die zahlungskräftigen Gäste mit ihrem Personal wohnten. Je weiter das 19. Jahrhundert voranschritt, desto mehr Sommerfrischler kamen, und diese gehörten schon bald nicht mehr nur dem Adel, sondern auch dem (Groß-)Bürgertum an. Neben Doberan und Heiligendamm wurden auch die benachbarten Orte zu beliebten Sommerzielen. Zwischen den Weltkriegen waren die Strände mit Urlaubern fast aller Gesellschaftsschichten gefüllt; ab 1933 wurde jüdischen Gästen der Aufenthalt jedoch zunehmend verwehrt. Spätestens ab den 1960ern überrollten die DDR-Bürger die Ostseeküste und auch die Wende tat der Beliebtheit keinen Abbruch.

Bathing at the Holy Dam

With the Reformation and the subsequent conflicts, the decline of the Doberan monastery and the surrounding area began. While the church survived as an evangelical place of worship, many other buildings in the complex fell into disrepair, and the village suffered through wars and epidemics. It was not until 1793/94 that Doberan regained its importance as a residence, becoming a town in 1879 and a designated "bath" in 1929.

The trigger for this development was the recommendation of the ducal physician that, for health reasons, one should bathe in the sea and therefore build a bathhouse at the Heiligen Damm. Heiligendamm, as the place was later called, became the first German seaside resort in 1793. Duke Friedrich Franz I, however, wanted to devote himself not only to his health but also to pleasure and had a summer residence built in neighboring Doberan.

In Heiligendamm, a unique classical-romantic total work of art consisting of bath and guest houses grew until 1870, which for decades attracted the European nobility, including the Russian imperial family, and is now known again as the "White Town by the Sea". In 2007, it was the venue for the G8 summit. The center of the ensemble has been the Kurhaus (spa house) with the ballroom, now a restaurant in the Grand Hotel. Adjacent to it is the former bathhouse, today integrated into the Grand Hotel as the House of Mecklenburg. To the west are the Burg Hohenzollern, also belonging to the Grand Hotel, and three cottages in the English country house style, today apartment buildings or still in need of repair. To the east of the Kurhaus, eight guest houses were built, which are now partially renovated and used as private and tourist apartments. The colonnades, built as a row of shops, are privately owned, while the orangery is used by the Grand Hotel.

Construction also took also place in Doberan, including the current Kurhaus, the former residence for the ducal family and later the administrative building, the salon building, a now-lost theater, two pavilions in the Chinese style, the Grand Ducal Palace, the Stahlbad sanatorium (later Moorbad, now a ruin), and the Prince's Palace. Several buildings were built in the neo-Gothic style, including the current Town Museum (constructed in 1887/88) and the gymnasium.

In the early years, the guests stayed in Doberan and only went to Heiligendamm to bathe. Of course, it was not just a matter of "jumping in the water". Ladies and gentlemen were assigned separate areas, and it was common to be transported a few meters into the sea in bathing carts and then get in the water from a small staircase. Entertainment was also part of the stay: the journey by coach, the socializing, walks, concerts, and boat rides. Back in Doberan, afternoons were spent on walks over the Kamp, a visit to the casino or the fashion shops. The evenings were devoted to the theater, balls, or social gatherings.

Cottages, hotels, guest and boarding houses were also quickly built in Heiligendamm, where financially secure guests and their staff lived. As the 19th century progressed, more and more summer visitors came, and these no longer belonged only to the nobility but also to the (upper) middle classes. In addition to Doberan and Heiligendamm, the neighboring towns also became popular summer destinations. Between the two World Wars, the beaches were filled with vacationers from almost all social classes; however, from 1933 onwards, Jewish guests were increasingly denied a stay. At the latest from the 1960s, East German citizens seeking recreation flooded the Baltic coast and the reunification did not diminish the popularity.

Seiten 56/57: Blick auf Heiligendamm Pages 56/57: View of Heiligendamm

Die geniale Lage von Heiligendamm ist offensichtlich, das Panorama grandios, der Einklang mit der Natur, insbesondere dem Meer, nicht zu übersehen – sei es bei Haus Mecklenburg (oben) oder bei der Villa Perle – Großfürstin Marie (Seite 59).

The brilliant position of Heiligendamm is obvious, its panorama magnificent, its harmony with nature undeniable, especially with the sea, for instance, at the mansions Haus Mecklenburg (page 58) or Villa Perle – Großfürstin Marie (at the top).

Die Seebrücke von Heiligendamm reicht 200 Meter in die Ostsee und bietet einen traumhaften Blick auf das Ensemble aus Grandhotel, Kurhaus und umliegenden Villen.

The "Seebrücke" (pier) in Heiligendamm extends 200 meters into the Baltic Sea and offers a gorgeous view of the ensemble of the grand hotel, the Kurhaus (spa building) and the surrounding mansion.

Seiten 62/63: Kurhaus, Haus Mecklenburg und im Hintergrund die Burg Hohenzollern – sie alle gehören zum Grand Hotel Heiligendamm.

Pages 62/63: Kurhaus, Haus Mecklenburg and Burg Hohenzollern (castle Hohenzollern) in the back. They all belong to the Grand Hotel Heiligendamm.

HEIC TE LAETITIA INVITAT POST BALNEA SANUM

Die Landschaft – geformt von Eiszeit und Gottes Hand

Vom Urwald, wie es ihn in Mecklenburg bis ins 12. Jahrhundert gab, ist heute nichts mehr erhalten. Als das Land deutsches Herzogtum wurde, begann die Zeit der großen Rodungen: Neben den alten slawischen Siedlungen entstanden deutsche Dörfer; moderne Landwirtschaft hielt Einzug, Kohlemeiler verschlangen ebenso wie die Feuer der zahlreichen Ziegeleien Unmengen alter Bäume.

Auch rings um das Doberaner Kloster wurden Wälder gerodet und Sümpfe entwässert. Viehweiden, Äcker und Obstgärten entstanden, auch Fischteiche, die zum Teil noch immer bewirtschaftet werden – wenn auch längst nicht mehr von Zisterziensermönchen. Bis heute prägen weite Felder die Landschaft, kleine Waldstücke, von denen die Kühlung westlich und der Gespensterwald östlich von Heiligendamm die bekanntesten sind, sorgen für Akzente.

Der Gespensterwald verdankt seinen Namen den bizarren Baumformen, die sich vor allem im Herbst und Winter blattlos schaurig-schön präsentieren. Unmittelbar an der Küste gelegen, tun hindurchziehende Nebel ein Übriges. Ein besonders spektakulärer, etwa 100 Meter tiefer Streifen mit bis zu 180 Jahre alten Eichen, Buchen, Eschen und Hainbuchen erstreckt sich entlang einer rund 1,3 Kilometer langen Steilküste. Das Ensemble bildet regelmäßig die Kulisse für Filmszenen, die irgendwo in Norddeutschland spielen und einer gewissen naturnahen Dramatik bedürfen.

„Kühlung" ist der Name eines bewaldeten Höhenzugs nahe Kühlunsgborn. Die Bezeichnung rührt von den „Kuhlen" her, den Senken des stark zerklüfteten Nordhangs. Gemeinsam mit dem rund 128 Meter hohen Diedrichshäger Berg kündet die Gegend von den geologischen Aktivitäten der Eiszeit vor rund 15000 Jahren.

Der Ortsname Heiligendamm leitet sich vom Heiligen Damm ab, der in einer Nacht des Jahres 1427 entstanden sein soll: Die Doberaner Mönche und ihre Bauern machten sich bei einer mehrtägigen Sturmflut daran, dem Meer einen Wall aus Steinen und Holz entgegenzustellen. Alle Anstrengung nützte jedoch nichts, die Wellen kamen näher. In höchster Not riefen die Mönche ihren Herrn an. Von Gottes Hand gelenkt drehte der Wind, und das Meer gebar in der Nacht unter unglaublichem Getöse einen gewaltigen Steindamm. Als Mönche und Bauern am Morgen zur wieder beruhigten Ostsee gingen, sahen sie das Wunder und nannten den Ort fortan Heiliger Damm.

Auch der Name des Conventer Sees geht auf das Kloster Doberan zurück. Er war ursprünglich eine Meeresbucht, die allmählich verlandete. Der so entstandene See wurde durch die Mönche bewirtschaftet, die Bezeichnung „Convent" steht für eine Versammlung von ihnen. Das Gewässer ist heute Kernstück der etwa 1200 Hektar großen Conventer Niederung, von der seit 1939 rund 200 Hektar unter Naturschutz stehen. Allerdings haben moderne Landwirtschaft, Melioration und das Einleiten von Abwässern dem Conventer See und der gesamten Niederung seit den 1950er-Jahren geschadet. Einer umfassenden Renaturierung stehen gegenwärtig Hochwasserschutzmaßnahmen entgegen. Trotzdem beheimatet die Gegend eine außerordentlich reiche Vogelwelt, vor allem das Vorkommen von Wasservögeln ist von Bedeutung. Das Naturschutzgebiet ist eines ihrer wichtigsten Brut- und Rastgebiete an der Küste.

The landscape – shaped by the ice age and God's hand

Of the primeval forest, as it existed in Mecklenburg until the 12th century, nothing remains today. When the land became a German duchy, the time of large clearings began: German villages sprang up next to the old Slavic settlements; modern agriculture was introduced, charcoal kilns and the fires of numerous brickworks consumed vast quantities of old trees.

Forests were also cleared and swamps drained around the Doberan monastery. Cattle pastures, fields and orchards were created, as well as fish ponds, some of which are still being farmed – albeit not by Cistercian monks anymore. To this day, wide fields characterize the landscape, and small patches of forest, of which the "Kühlung" west and the ghost forest east of Heiligendamm are the best known, provide accents.

The ghost forest owes its name to the bizarre shapes of the trees, which present themselves as eerily beautiful without leaves, especially in autumn and winter. Located directly on the coast, the fog that passes through does the rest. The approximately 100-meter-deep strip of up to 180-year-old oaks, beeches, ash trees and hornbeams stretches along an approximately 1.3-kilometer-long cliff. The ensemble regularly forms the backdrop for film scenes set somewhere in northern Germany and requiring a certain natural drama.

"Kühlung" is the name of a forested mountain range near Kühlunsgborn. The name comes from the "Kuhlen", the depressions of the strongly rugged northern slope. Together with the approximately 128-meter-high Diedrichshäger Berg, the area bears witness to the geological activities of the ice age around 15000 years ago.

The place name Heiligendamm is derived from the Holy Dam, which is said to have been created one night in 1427: The Doberan monks and their farmers set about building a rampart of stones and wood against the sea during a storm surge that lasted several days. However, all efforts were of no avail, the waves came closer. In the greatest distress, the monks called upon their Lord. Guided by God's hand, the wind turned, and the sea gave birth to a huge stone dam during the night with an incredible roar. When monks and farmers went to the calmed Baltic Sea in the morning, they saw the miracle and called the place Holy Dam from then on.

The name of Lake Convent also goes back to the Doberan monastery. It was originally a sea bay that gradually silted up. The resulting lake was farmed by the Cistercians, and the name "Convent" stands for an assembly of monks. Today, the lake is the core of the Convent lowland, which covers about 1200 hectares and of which about 200 hectares have been under nature protection since 1939. However, modern agriculture, melioration and the discharge of sewage have damaged the lake and the entire lowland since the 1950s. Flood control measures currently stand in the way of comprehensive renaturation. Nevertheless, the area is home to an exceptionally rich bird life, especially the occurrence of waterfowl is of importance. The nature reserve is one of their most important breeding and resting areas on the coast.

In der Abendsonne leuchten Steilküste und Strand besonders schön. Aber nicht immer ist die Ostsee so ruhig!
The steep coast and the beach glow most beautifully in the setting sun. But the Baltic Sea is not always this calm!

Ob vom Gespensterwald in Nienhagen aus oder direkt am Strand: Die Küste bei Heiligendamm bietet häufig eine magische Atmosphäre – nicht nur kurz vor dem Sonnenuntergang.

From the Gespensterwald (Ghost Forest) in Nienhagen or directly at the beach: The coast at Heiligendamm frequently presents a magical atmosphere – not only at sunset.

39
38

H

OSTSEE
KÜHLUNGSBORN-
WEST
OST
HEILIGENDAMM
Der heilige Damm
Nienhagen
Nienhäger Holz
(Gespensterwald)
Börgerende
Rethwisch
Conventer See
Doberaner Wiesen
Großer Wohld
Kleiner Wohld
Riedensee
Kägsdorf
Klein Bollhagen
Wittenbeck
Hinter Bollhagen
Molli-Bahn
Pferderenn-bahn
Bastorf
KÜHLUNG
Mechelsdorf
Wichmannsdorf
RERIK
Neu Gaarz
Hohen Niendorf
129
Diedrichshagener Berg
Diedrichshagen
Steffenshagen
Walkenhagen
Doberaner Holz
Kellers Wald
nach ROSTOCK
BAD DOBERAN
Althof
WUSTROW
Wustrow
Blengow
Jennewitz
Reddelich
SALZHAFF
Biendorf
Roggow
KRÖPELIN
Glashagen
Hohenfelde
Hütter Wohld
Teßmannsdorf
Retschow
Pepelow
Rakow
Hanstorf
NEUBUKOW
Boiensdorf
105/E22
Blowatz
nach WISMAR
Legende
0
2,5
5
7,5
10 km
Ortschaft
Bundesstraße
wichtige Land- oder Ortsstraße
Eisenbahn mit Bahnhof
Mecklenburgische Bäderbahn mit Bahnhof ("Molli")
Wald
See/Fluß
Karte nicht maßstabsgerecht
C.T.